D0661817

Skinny Bitchin'

Skinny Bitchin'

*A "Get Off Your Ass" Journal
to Help You Change Your Life,
Achieve Your Goals, and
Rock Your World!*

by Rory Freedman and Kim Barnouin

RUNNING PRESS
PHILADELPHIA · LONDON

9   8   7   6   5   4   3   2   1
Digit on the right indicates the number of this printing

Library of Congress Control Number: 2008937013

ISBN 978-0-7624-3537-1

Cover and interior design by Maria Taffera Lewis
Edited by Jennifer Kasius
Typography: Bauer Bodoni and Dutch 801

Running Press Book Publishers
2300 Chestnut Street
Philadelphia, PA 19103-4371

Visit us on the web!
www.runningpress.com

Dedication

For Dr. Wayne Dyer, Shakti Gawain, Louise Hay,
Tony Robbins, Sue Foley, Jackie Poper, Lauren Silverman,
Tracy Silverman, and Keesha Whitehurst—
with love and gratitude for the profound and indelible
effects you have each had and continue to have on our lives.

Introduction

We can clearly mark the time in our lives when we suddenly knew that we could do, have, experience, accomplish, and feel more. We were each trudging along, minding our own business when books by Dr. Wayne Dyer fell from the sky. Not too long after, the work of Tony Robbins also appeared. Soon after reading their books and listening to their CDs, we believed in ourselves and the universe enough to know that there was more for us than working three jobs and struggling to get by (Kim) and an unfulfilling career that included commuting three hours a day and working eight (Rory). Suddenly, we had all the confidence in the world that we could have and do and be anything we wanted. Anything. It didn't take long for us to realize that what we wanted more than anything else was to be of service. We wanted to make a real difference. From there, *Skinny Bitch* was born.

Suddenly, a high school dropout was earning a Master of Science degree in Holistic Nutrition and doing in-depth research (Kim). And a big-mouthed troublemaker who had paid friends to pen her college papers was writing (Rory). There was no reason to think that we would be successful in securing a literary agent or a publishing deal or that our book would ever be a success. But from day one, we believed in its inherent value and we literally spoke the book into existence. Using the tools we learned from Dr. Wayne Dyer, Tony Robbins, and others like them, we created something where there was nothing. And we envisioned the path our success would take, long before it took shape.

The teachings we've learned have altered the course of each of our lives. We feel as though we were sleepwalking previously—that we were on autopilot. And now that we're awake, our lives are infinitely more purposeful, powerful, and miraculous. Before, we had no idea that the universe wants us all to succeed. That there is enough abundance in this world for everyone. That anything and everything is possible. Now that we know this with every fiber of our beings, we want to share it with you.

So we're giving you Bitches some homework. For whatever reason, there is magic in journaling. There's just something about writing your fears, your gripes, your goals—it can't be explained. All we know is that we are living proof that it is effective beyond measure. So every day, from now on (or until you feel like every aspect of your life is so friggin' amazing you just can't stand it), we want you to journal. On the following pages, you'll find some of our favorite motivational quotes that you can meditate on throughout the day, suggestions for ways to shake things up in your own lives, and enough blank space to do your thing.

We want you to do, have, experience, accomplish, and feel everything life has to offer. We want you to stretch and grow and be who you were born to be. We want every day of your lives to be exhilarating, breathtaking, and awe-inspiring.

We want you to blow your own minds and to rock your own worlds!

What have you failed at in the past that you now regret? Or what task, project, or goal are you avoiding because it's challenging?
Today, start taking it on.
And this time, don't be such a pussy when things get tough.

"When everything seems to be going against you, remember that the airplane takes off against the wind, not with it."

—*Henry Ford*

Know this and be okay with it:

Not everyone is going to like you.

Write a love letter to each of your parents
(or someone who was like a parent to you)
thanking them for everything
they've ever done for you.
(These letters make great gifts for birthdays,
Mother's Day, and Father's Day.)

Plan a party. Seriously.
Start planning it right now.
Live a little.

Write a letter to yourself explaining why you are so beautiful, special, and worthy of love.

You yourself, as much as anybody
in the entire universe,
deserves your love and affection.

—*Buddha*

Try meditating today.
Do your best to let your mind
"turn off" and be still.

"Life is either a daring adventure
 or nothing."

—*Helen Keller*

Today, say "yes" to things that are totally outside your comfort zone. This is your life! What are you waiting for?

Make a list of people who have
wrong you and write out
the ways in which they did so.
When you're done,
try and see things from their point
of view, and write in their defense.

"How people treat you is their karma;
how you react is yours."

—*Dr. Wayne Dyer*

Make a list of ways you can be of service to others today—
how you can help out a friend, a neighbor, or even a stranger.
Then, when you carry out your good deeds, tell no one.
See how good it feels, even if no one else recognizes you
for your kindness.

"Real integrity is doing the right thing, knowing that nobody's going to know whether you did it or not."

—*Oprah Winfrey*

"You are never asked to do
more than you are able
without being given the
strength and ability to do it."

—*Eileen Caddy*

Feeling sorry for yourself?
Have at it. Bask in your misery
for a solid fifteen minutes.
But then get it together and
cut the shit! Life's too short.
Deal with what's ailing you
and put it behind you.

Spend the day outside
communing with nature.
Seriously. It's like pushing
a reset button on your mind
and wiping away all the crazy.

"In an ugly and unhappy world
the richest man can purchase nothing
but ugliness and unhappiness."

—*George Bernard Shaw*

Do you want to be rich (and famous)?
Sort out why it seems so important.
Then dig deep and find out
what really, truly matters most to you.

Explore the fact that specific physical attributes are considered more attractive than others and how and why this came to be. Get to the point where you can see what a huge, steaming pile of bullshit it is. Be grateful for the body you have, exactly as it is. (Just be sure to treat it like a temple: eat right and exercise, duh!)

"How poor are they that have not patience.
What wound did ever heal but by degrees?"

—*William Shakespeare*

In this fast-paced day and age,
most of us act like impatient assholes.
Take your time today—
with everything you do.

Pay attention to the negative effects certain foods have on your body, moods, and energy level. You could even start a separate little food journal, recording what you eat and drink throughout the day and how you feel as a result. This way, when you start making positive changes to your diet, you'll appreciate all of the results— not just the weight loss.

Make a list of your heroes and the qualities
they possess that make them who they are.
Then try to emulate those qualities
throughout the day.

"Sooner or later, those who win
are those who think they can."

—*Richard Bach*

Are you a pussy?

Stand up for yourself today.

Are you a bully? Be gentle today.

"Life shrinks or expands
in proportion to one's courage."

—*Anaïs Nin*

Tell someone how you really feel, flirt shamelessly,
or let someone know if they've stepped on your toes.
Don't worry about the outcome. Just be brave.

Whom do you admire and why?
Tell him or her in person,
on the phone, or via email.

"Whatever you can do or dream you can, begin it. Boldness has genius, magic and power in it. Begin it."

—*Goethe*

You know what you've been dying to do
but you've been putting off…

Do it!

Today, catch yourself looking
for opportunities to be
offended and figure out
why in the hell you'd want
to be bothered by someone
or something.

Just for today, try not to care about how you look. Wear whatever you want, don't obsess about your hair, and detach your sense of self from your appearance.

"Begin to see yourself as a soul with a body
rather than a body with a soul."

—*Dr. Wayne Dyer*

Go seven
consecutive days
without watching
TV or surfing the
Internet.
See how it
changes your life.

"Many people pray and receive
the answers to their prayers, but ignore them
or deny them, because the answers
didn't come in the expected form."

—Sophy Burnham

Are you living in the truth?

Like really, truly, seriously living in the truth?

Make a list of all the red flags you've been ignoring in your life.

Um, hello?
Do you think you get
to go back
and do things over?
You don't.
So start living your life large
this very friggin' second!

The only way to live
is by accepting each minute
as an unrepeatable miracle."

—*Storm Jamesson*

"So many people tiptoe through life,
so carefully, to arrive, safely, at death."

—*Jermaine Evans*

Write down your biggest fears
and why you think they have
such a hold on you.
On paper, get mad that they've
kept you from really living.
With your written words,
permanently banish them
from your mind and your life.

Do what you have to do
to love where you live.
Clean, redecorate, buy flowers,
burn incense, and light candles—
whatever it takes to make
your home feel joyful and peaceful.

Don't expect those around you
to "get" what you're all about.
Provided you're not being a stupid asshole,
know that you're just fine the way you are.

"Great spirits have always encountered violent opposition from mediocre minds."

—*Albert Einstein*

"Being deeply loved by someone gives you strength; loving someone deeply gives you courage."

—*Lao Tzu*

Are you holding back in your
relationship or avoiding
getting into one because of old
injuries or fear of getting hurt?

Well, knock it off.

Today, with your partner,
practice true, pure, unconditional,
unbridled, crazy-ass love.
If you're single,
figure out what you're afraid of.

Remember when
you were little
and you colored
just because?
Color, draw, doodle,
whatever.
But do something
here and now
on these pages to tap
into your inner child.

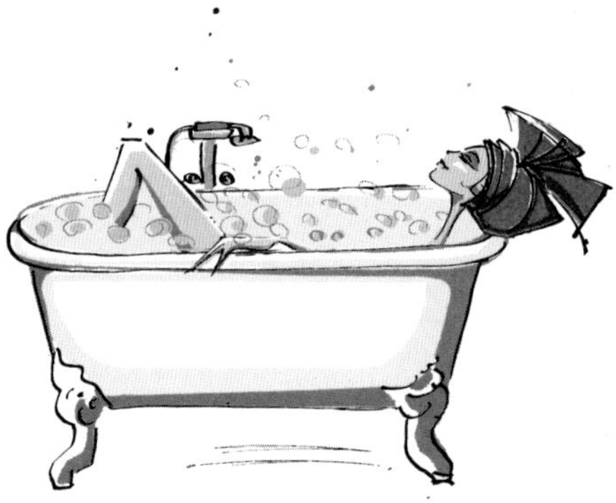

Do something generous
for yourself today.
Get a massage,
buy yourself
something frivolous,
eat something decadent.

"Our greatest glory
   is not in never falling,
   but in rising
   every time we fall."

—*Confucius*

You know how you feel vulnerable and exposed
sharing stories of failure? Do it anyway—
humbling experiences make for great growth spurts.
Tell someone (not your best friend)
about a time you made a complete fool of yourself
And feel okay while you're telling your tale.

Which of your character defects would you most like to change?
Today, be hyper-conscious of it and do your best to address it.
(But don't beat yourself up for being human!)

"Pain is temporary. Quitting lasts forever."

—*Lance Armstrong*

Get your fat ass off the couch and get to the gym, go for a hike, or
go ride a bike. Push yourself today (in a healthy, safe way).

"When challenge is present,
the teacher is in the room."

—Anonymous

Is there a relationship in your life that just isn't working?

What would it take to repair it?

If it's irreparable, unhealthy, and unfulfilling,

what would it take for you to end it?

Quit "saving"
your fancy underwear
for a special day.
Today is that day!
Wear 'em!

Tackle the task
you've been putting off
that's cluttering your mental
and physical space.

"Leap and the net will appear."

—*John Burroughs*

I (Rory) was so inspired
by this quote that I quit my
six-figure-a-year job to become
an animal rights activist.
I didn't have a job lined up or
anything else figured out.
I just believed that
"the net" would appear.
It didn't materialize
the moment I wanted it to
or how I envisioned it,
but when it did appear,
it wound up being
even better than
I'd originally hoped.

"Let thy food be thy medicine
and thy medicine be thy food."

—*Hippocrates*

Get your head out of your ass and go read *Skinny Bitch*.
(If you've already read it, conjure up your perfect week of eating,
go to the grocery store, and make it happen this week.)

"From what we get, we can make a living;
what we give, however, makes a life."

—*Arthur Ashe*

Do the research and legwork today
so that you can commit
to volunteering for a worthy cause
some time in the next thirty days.

Play hooky from work today and spend the day
doing something you really love.

And do not feel guilty!

"How am I going to live today in order to create the tomorrow I'm committed to?"

—*Tony Robbins*

On one of his CDs,
Tony suggests the following:
Write down three goals
that you'd like to accomplish
in three years or less.
Now don't get up
from the table until you do
something tangible towards
accomplishing each
of the three goals.
This really, really works.
How do we know?
"Write a book called *Skinny Bitch*"
was once written on a goal list.

Make a list of all the hardships
you've endured throughout your life.
Next, make a list of all the upcoming
problems you're anticipating.
Then, write about how your strength,
determination, and spirit got you
through the rough patches
in the past and how they'll serve you
again in the future.

"What lies behind us and what lies before us
are tiny matters compared to what lies within us."

—*Ralph Waldo Emerson*

"There is nothing that you cannot be,
or do, or have."

—*Esther and Jerry Hicks*

Today, spend at least fifteen minutes journaling about what you want to be, do, or have. When you're done, spend ten minutes sitting in silence, eyes closed, focused on what you want.

Why don't you believe good things can happen to you?
What do you have to release in order to know
that you are entitled to love, happiness, and prosperity?

"The universe is designed to give us
everything we need and want.
It's really our own fears and our feelings of
unworthiness, shame, and doubt
that keep us from receiving
the incredible abundance and fullness
and goodness of life."

—*Shakti Gawain*

Write about a time
when you were
painfully embarrassed—
when you were sure
you'd rather die
than live with
the mortification.
Then, write
what beautiful
and powerful lesson
you learned
from the experience.

Practice being your unabashed self today
and loving every second of it.

"Be who you are and say what you feel
because those who mind don't matter
and those who matter don't mind."

—*Dr. Seuss*

"One who fears failure limits his activities.
Failure is only the opportunity
to more intelligently begin again."

—*Henry Ford*

Yeah, admitting fault
is scary and weird
and uncomfortable.
Too bad.
Do you owe someone
an apology?
Write out what you'll say
and then get on it!
Today is the perfect day
to make amends.

Know with every
fiber and cell
of your being
that today
you wish
to put
only pure,
beautiful,
healthful foods
in your body.

"With courage you will dare to take risks,
have the strength to be compassionate
and the wisdom to be humble.
Courage is the foundation of integrity."

—*Keshavan Nair*

Do something really courageous today.
Don't care about how you come across.
Whatever scares you, fight against it.

Just be brave.

Make a list of everything you want in a life partner.
Now make a list of all the ways you need to behave
in order to attract someone like this.
(For example, you can't expect to land a mate
who's good with money while you're out
running up your credit cards and shopping recklessly.)

"If one desires a change,
one must be that change
before that change
can take place."

—*Gita Bellin*

Do you identify with
your physical appearance
a little too much?
Or, conversely,
do you neglect your looks?
This week, do the opposite!
If you always sex it up,
go casual/comfortable
for seven days.
And learn how to live
as a being, and not
a piece of ass.
If you usually look
like a bag of shit,
get it together
for seven days.
Love yourself enough
to think you deserve
to look good.

Take a yoga class this week.

"Without rain, nothing grows."

—*Anonymous*

Some of the most painful experiences in our lives
have provided us with the most profound
and important lessons.
So don't run or hide from the pain.
Know that something magnificent awaits you
on the other side of it.

Do something today
to honor your creative side,
whether it be painting,
singing, dancing,
drawing, writing,
taking pictures—
whatever makes you
feel alive!

I (Kim) spent many years
moving from place to place,
thinking relocating
would solve my problems.
After reading this quote,
it finally occurred to me:
"The common denominator
in all my problems is me."
What are your issues
that you take with you
 everywhere you go?

"No matter where you go, there you are."

—*Confucius*

"In any given moment,

the universe is primed

to give us new life,

to begin again,

to create new opportunities,

to miraculously heal situations,

to change all darkness to light

and fear to love."

—*Marianne Williamson*

What one thing have you done
that you won't let yourself
off the hook for?
Write all the terrible things
you associate with it.
Then, write yourself a good excuse
for your behavior and forgive yourself.
(If you need to apologize to someone
to absolve yourself, now's the time.)

"For me there are only two types of women: goddesses and doormats."

—*Pablo Picasso*

If you are or have ever been
a doormat, journal about it.
By the time you're done writing,
you better be a f**king goddess!

"God grant me the serenity
to accept the things I cannot change;
Courage to change the things I can;
And wisdom to know the difference."

—*Reinhold Niebuhr*

Being descriptive as to why,
write down your pet peeves about your
close friends or family members.
Then try and figure out what these
annoyances say about **you**.

"Knowledge of what is possible
is the beginning of happiness."

—*George Santayana*

Make a list of all the good things that have happened
to everyone you know. Realize that miracles are abundant
and are always looking for a place to land.

"Just when the
caterpillar thought
its life was over,
it became a butterfly."

—*Anonymous*

When we first came up with *Skinny Bitch*, we met with three different imprints at a major publishing company—all three turned us down, and we were devastated. But then, we got our shot with a publisher we had never heard of. And look us at now! In your life, what might look like the end but may eventually give way to something promising?

Wear something today
you would usually never —
something that
you've wanted to wear,
but never dared.
See it as a metaphor
for something bigger in your life.

"You must do the thing you think you cannot do."

—*Eleanor Roosevelt*

"In the middle of difficulty lies opportunity."

—*Albert Einstein*

Don't run from conflict, challenge,
or discomfort. Face it head on.

Stop yourself from giving
unsolicited advice today.
Just listen and commiserate.
You don't have all the answers.

You know that guy you've been obsessing over for three years who's just not that into you? He's an axe murderer. So thank the universe for looking out for you and move on. Make a list of all the things you know suck about him (but were unwilling to admit to yourself).

"Remember that not getting what you want
is sometimes a wonderful stroke of luck."

—*The Dalai Lama*

"People say that you're going the wrong way when it's simply a way of your own."

—*Angelina Jolie*

What does your path look like?
Or better yet, what **should** your path look like?

"Whatever the present
moment contains,
accept it as if
you had chosen it.
Always work with it,
not against it."

—*Eckhart Tolle*

What good does it do
to complain, pout, or
wish things were different?
Whether you're taking out
the trash, stuck in traffic, or
bogged down with work,
embrace every present
moment today
and do your best
to enjoy each one.

Make a list of five super-empowering affirmations and commit
to reading them aloud morning, noon, and night for a whole week.
For example: "I am a beautiful person," "I am financially secure,"
or "I am healthy and whole"—whatever **you** need to affirm.

"The moment you say affirmations,
you are stepping out of the victim role.
You are no longer helpless.
You are acknowledging your own power."

—*Louise Hay*

"There is but one cause of human failure.
And that is man's lack of faith in his true Self."

—*William James*

What activity have you always wanted to try
but never gotten around to? Today, make concrete plans to do it!

"We are still masters of our fate.
We are still captains of our souls."

—*Winston Churchill*

Enroll a friend and do this together:
Today, each time you catch yourself
saying something mean or
negative about yourself,
immediately stop yourself and
say something positive instead.
(You'll be shocked at how often you belittle yourself.)
Keep a tally of every time you
almost said something mean.
When the day is over, for every mean thing
you were going to say about yourself,
give your friend a buck.

"I stand for freedom of expression,
doing what you believe in,
and going after your dreams."

—*Madonna*

Seriously, by far,
the coolest thing
about Madonna:
She does whatever
the fuck she wants and
never apologizes for it.
Find your inner Madonna today
and see how long
you can keep her around.

"Don't compromise yourself. You are all you've got."

—*Janis Joplin*

Journal about a time
when you were inauthentic or
you sold yourself out.

"Life is about creating new opportunities,
not waiting for them to come to you."

—*Salma Hayek*

Well, don't just sit there looking stupid—
what opportunity do you want
to create for yourself
within the next thirty days?

"Ninety percent of life is just showing up."

—*Woody Allen*

There's an ebb and flow to life.
And sometimes, you just aren't feeling it.
As long as your blah days
are few and far between,
feel free to honor them.
You don't need to be Supergirl
or a goddess today. Just show up.

Write three tangible
things you can do
to make your life
satisfying.

"Open your eyes and look within.
Are you satisfied with the life you're living?"

—*Bob Marley*

Today, be patient with and kind to everyone you encounter.
Make a list of people who will present a challenge,
and figure out how you will be patient with and kind to even them.

"Be kind, for everyone you meet
is fighting a hard battle."

—*Philo*

Start getting serious about making positive changes to your lifestyle. Set mini-goals for yourself and tackle them one at a time. Spend a week removing one dirty vice item (booze, coffee, soda, meat, dairy, etc.). Dedicate the week to getting this vice out of your diet, your body, your kitchen, and your mind.

"No one can make you feel
  inferior without your consent."

—*Eleanor Roosevelt*

Who do you shrink around and why?

Often in life, we don't get what we want because we aren't clear on what it is we actually want. Get clear here and now. The universe will respond.

"To reach a port we must sail—
sail, not tie at anchor—sail, not drift."

—*Franklin Roosevelt*

"We must become the change
we wish to see in the world."

—*Mahatma Gandhi*

Make a list of what people can do to make the world a better place. Now imagine what the world would be like if **you** were your best, highest self. What do you need to do to be that person?

"Think occasionally of the suffering
of which you spare yourself the sight."

—*Albert Schweitzer*

How can you call yourself
an "animal lover,"
and then contribute to the torture
and slaughter of animals,
just so you can eat and wear them?
There's no integrity in that.
Start investigating
vegetarianism today.
(Visit GoVeg.com
for a free vegetarian starter kit.)

Smile and say "hello" to everyone you pass today.
Go one step further and have meaningful interactions and
conversations with everyone you encounter.
Be generous with yourself in both speaking and listening.

'The true measure of a man is how he treats someone who can do him absolutely no good."

—*Samuel Johnson*

"A man is a success if he gets up in the morning and gets to bed at night, and in between he does what he wants to do."

—*Bob Dylan*

If you're being completely honest
with yourself, what do you really want
to be or do in this lifetime?

"Lost time is never
found again."

—*Benjamin Franklin*

Are you estranged from a family member or friend?
Write down what happened to cause the rift
from your side, then approach it from his or hers.
Then ask yourself: "Is it more important
for me to be 'right' than to be at peace?"
If the answer is "yes," you're a jackass.
Patch that shit up!

"Every human being is the author
of his own health or disease."

—*Buddha*

Get clear:
Are you living your life
as someone who is healthy,
happy, and vibrant
or someone who is
sick, angry, and sad?
If it's the latter,
it's because you're being a victim.

Knock it off!

The best way to turn
that shit around
is to make a list of all the things
in your life you are grateful for.
Every single one of them.
Bask in your gratitude all day long.

Get over the notion that, "If my ass was higher…
if my stomach was flatter… if my thighs were thinner…
then I'd be happy." Make a list of all the things you love
about your body. And really mean it.

"Have no fear of perfection. You'll never reach it."

—*Salvador Dali*

Get the book *The Artist's Way* by Julia Cameron and start it today. Watch your life transform!

Go back and read all that you wrote
since you started this journal.
Reflect on who you were,
who you are,
and who you want to be.

What do you still need to do?

What are you waiting for?